Just Enough
Difficult Topics
Made Easy

What Happens When A Loved One Dies?

Our First Talk About Death

Dr. Jillian Roberts

illustrated by

Cindy Revell

ORCA BOOK PUBLISHERS

Text copyright © Jillian Roberts 2016, 2022
Illustrations copyright © Cindy Revell 2016, 2022

Published in Canada and the United States in 2022 by Orca Book Publishers.
Previously published in 2016 by Orca Book Publishers as a hardcover
(ISBN 9781459809451) and available as an ebook (ISBN 9781459809468, PDF;
ISBN 9781459809475, EPUB).
orcabook.com

Library and Archives Canada Cataloguing in Publication
Title: What happens when a loved one dies? : our first talk about
death / Dr. Jillian Roberts ; illustrated by Cindy Revell.
Names: Roberts, Jillian, 1971- author. | Revell, Cindy, illustrator.
Series: Roberts, Jillian, 1971- Just enough.
Description: Series statement: Just enough: difficult
topics made easy | Previously published: 2016.
Identifiers: Canadiana 20210169206 | ISBN 9781459831858 (softcover)
Subjects: LCSH: Death—Juvenile literature. | LCSH: Bereavement—Juvenile
literature. | LCSH: Grief—Juvenile literature. | LCSH: Children and death.
Classification: LCC HQ1073.3 .R63 2022 | DDC j306.9—dc23

Library of Congress Control Number: 2021934727

Summary: A nonfiction picture book that introduces very young children to
the concept of death in a way that is gentle, age-appropriate and comforting.

Orca Book Publishers is committed to reducing the consumption
of nonrenewable resources in the making of our books. We make
every effort to use materials that support a sustainable future.

Orca Book Publishers gratefully acknowledges the support
for its publishing programs provided by the following
agencies: the Government of Canada, the Canada Council
for the Arts and the Province of British Columbia through
the BC Arts Council and the Book Publishing Tax Credit.

Cover and interior artwork by Cindy Revell

Printed and bound in South Korea.

25 24 23 22 • 1 2 3 4

For my godchildren.

—J.R.

For my grandparents, who gave me memories of lemon trees, peonies, patchwork quilts, tobacco shreds, warm hugs and love.

—C.R.

Everything in nature has a life that is meaningful and important.

The fish in the sea, the birds in the air and the animals in the forest are all alive.

All life is connected and serves a special purpose.
When a living thing reaches the end of its life, it dies.

When living things die, we call this *death*.

What does death mean?

Death means that a living thing is no longer alive. A tree full of leaves and blossoms is alive. An old tree that has fallen over in the forest is no longer alive. It is dead.

Do people die too?

Yes. People are living things. Our lives are also important, meaningful and connected. At the end of our lives we all die too—just like the old tree in the forest.

What happens when someone dies?

When someone dies, that person's body stops working.
People can die from old age, illness or even, sometimes,
an accident.

Those who knew and loved the person who died will often gather to say goodbye. Usually this is done at a ceremony, called a *funeral*.

Funerals often take place in spiritual places like churches, synagogues, mosques and temples.

What happens to the person who has died?
Where does that person go?

There are lots of different ideas about what happens after death. Many cultures believe that a person is made up of both a body and a *soul*, and that the soul lives on even though the body is no longer alive.

What is a soul?

A soul is what makes you who you are. It is the part of you
that loves others.

Where does the soul go after a person dies?

Many people believe that the soul journeys to the *afterlife* to join the souls of other people who have died.

What is the afterlife?

Many cultures think of the afterlife as a joyful and loving place where the soul lives forever. In some religions, this place is called *heaven*. Others believe that we are reborn or return to the earth in a different form.

Will I ever see the person I love again?

Death means that a person's body is no longer alive, so you won't see the person you love again. But that person can still live on in our memories, thoughts and even dreams. In this way, our loved ones are always a part of us.

Why do I feel so sad?

When someone dies, it's normal to be very sad and miss that person. It can be hard to say goodbye to someone you love.

What can I do to feel better?

While you may always miss the person who died, it can be helpful to do or make something special to celebrate your loved one. Remembering and honoring somebody's life can help us to move on after that person dies.

Death can be really hard to understand. There are lots of different ideas about what happens after we die, but nobody knows for sure.

We do know that it's something that connects us all.
And it's one of the great mysteries of life.

Just a Few More Questions

What happens to the body when someone dies?

We often think of people as having both a body and a soul, and no one knows for certain what happens to the soul after death. The body of a person who has died is often buried, or the body is turned to ash in a process called *cremation*. Whether a body is buried or cremated, the process is done in a careful and special way to celebrate the life of the deceased person. This is a sacred process in many cultures.

What is reincarnation?

Reincarnation is the belief that when someone dies, he or she returns to the earth in a different form. According to some cultures, a soul is on a journey to learn how to be good and wise, and it can take many lifetimes to learn the needed lessons. To these cultures, a soul is constantly growing and seeking goodness and truth.

What happens when a pet dies?

Pets can be very important members of the family, so it's normal to be sad when a pet dies. Just like a person's, the body of a pet can be buried or cremated. Some people believe that pets also go to heaven or are reincarnated. Other people believe that nature is a constant cycle of life and death, and that the bodies of animals become an important part of this cycle of nature.

What is grief?

Grief is the feeling of loss and sadness you have when a loved one dies. You can feel grief when a person dies or when a pet dies. It can be hard and painful, *but it is okay.* Grieving is an important part of being a person. By allowing yourself to grieve, you give your heart a chance to heal. Expressing your feelings helps you grieve. You can express your feelings by talking about them or writing them down, as well as through art and music. *It is okay to share your sad feelings with others.* It is important to remember that you are not alone and that you will not always feel so sad.